NEXT GENERATION INDIAN FOOD
Fusion Flavours of the Subcontinent

Murad Hossain

with Pauline Norris

© 2009 Murad Hossain
Next Generation Indian Food

ISBN 978-0-9564013-0-4

Published by Elma Publishing
3 East Row
Chichester
West Sussex
PO19 1PD

The right of Murad Hossain to be identified as the author of this work has been asserted by him in accordance with the Copyright, Designs and Patents Act 1988.

All rights reserved. No part of this publication may be produced in any form or by any means – graphic, electronic or mechanical including photocopying, recording, taping or information storage and retrieval systems – without the prior permission, in writing, of the publisher.

A CIP catalogue record of this book can be obtained from the British Library.

Photography by Peter Lincoln

Book designed by Michael Walsh at
THE BETTER BOOK COMPANY LIMITED
5 Lime Close
Chichester
PO19 6SW

and printed by
ASHFORD COLOUR PRESS
Unit 600 Fareham Reach
Fareham Road
Gosport
Hants PO13 0FW

Quail and Potato Curry
Recipe on page 26

CONTENTS

Starters 1

Soups 12

Fish 16

Meat/Poultry 26

Vegetables 40

Bread 46

Rice 48

Dessert 50

ACKNOWLEDGEMENTS

My mother Rahima Akter and my late father Mosharaf Hossain for all their encouragement

Pauline Norris for watching me cooking the recipes and helping to write this book

Joe Beaver, executive chef Marriott Hotel, London Heathrow

Philip Cooper, previously executive chef The Mirabelle, London

Gus Johnson for the basics of French cooking

Manjula Shacdev for training me as an Indian chef

Jahangir Hussain and Fakrul Islam, my business partners

All the staff of the Masala Gate Restaurant, Chichester

CHEF'S TIP: Make the rolls several hours before and keep in the fridge. The breadcrumbs stay on the roll better during deep-frying.

ALTERNATIVE FLAVOUR: Use half blue cheese and half Cheddar. Do NOT use any seasoning of salt with this version, as blue cheese is naturally salty.

Sag Roll

SPICY SPINACH AND POTATO ROLL
WITH CREAMY COCONUT SAUCE

*Preparation: 40 minutes Cooking: 30 minutes
Makes four rolls*

One of the most popular and delicious starters at Murad's restaurant is based on a recipe from his grandmother

Ingredients

The roll
- 350gm peeled potatoes
- 80gm mild Cheddar cheese
- 2 small shallots finely chopped
- 4 cloves of garlic finely chopped
- Vegetable oil
- 100gm fresh leaf spinach
- 1 egg
- Dried breadcrumbs
- Turmeric
- Dried coriander
- Dried cumin
- Garam masala
- Salt
- Fresh coriander

The sauce
- 50 gm butter or clarified ghee
- 85 gm desiccated coconut
- 1.5 tbs. sugar
- 350ml single cream

Chop the potatoes into chunks and boil in lightly salted water.

Heat a frying pan and gently brown two finely chopped garlic cloves in a little vegetable oil. Add the shallots and brown. Stir in a pinch of turmeric and dried coriander. Remove from the heat and add the fresh spinach with a splash of water. Season with salt. Return to the hob briefly and toss to wilt the spinach. Using the back of a metal spoon squeeze the spinach against the side of the pan and remove the excess water.

Strain the potatoes and mash until smooth. Gently fry two cloves of garlic in vegetable oil and add the mashed potato. Add $1/8^{th}$ tsp. turmeric, ½ tsp. dried coriander, $1/8^{th}$ tsp. cumin and a pinch of garam masala followed by a handful of coarsely chopped fresh coriander leaves and stir.

Assemble rolls by taking a ball of the potato mixture in the hand. Flatten it and place a quarter of the cheese and spinach mixture in the centre. Close the potato around the mixture so that it is concentrated in the centre of the ball. Repeat to form three more balls. Coat them in beaten egg and roll in the dried breadcrumbs. Place the balls in the fridge for at least 30 minutes.

In the meantime prepare the sauce. Melt the butter in a frying pan and gently sauté the coconut. Add the sugar and finally the cream. Gently simmer.

Deep-fry the spinach and potato rolls. Place on the plate, cover with the sauce and decorate with fresh coriander or mango coulis.

Goti Mahal

TOMATOES STUFFED WITH SPICY CHICKEN IN A GINGER AND TOMATO SAUCE

Preparation: 20 minutes   Cooking: 30 minutes   Makes four portions

This attractive, light starter is Murad's own recipe

Ingredients
- 5 tomatoes
- 1 small onion finely chopped
- 2 cloves garlic
- Small piece of chopped ginger root
- 1 tsp. turmeric
- 1 tsp. dried coriander
- 1 tsp. dried cumin
- Pinch garam masala
- 1 chicken breast finely chopped
- 150gm mild Cheddar cheese
- 1 tbs. plain flour

Sauce
- 1 clove garlic
- 1 tsp. chopped ginger root
- 2 tbs. tomato puree
- 1 tbs. tomato ketchup
- Pinch cumin
- Pinch chilli powder
- 1 tsp. oil and vinegar dressing
- Pinch sugar
- Fresh coriander
- 4 tbs. water

Blanch 4 tomatoes. Cut off the top of each tomato. Scoop out the pulp and retain.

Make some garlic and ginger paste by blending garlic and ginger root with a small amount of water and 1 tbs. oil. garlic & ginger paste recipe

Saute onion. Chop up fifth tomato and add to the onion with a tsp. of the garlic ginger paste. Add the spices, all the retained tomato pulp and a little water. Stir in the chicken and cook. Season to taste.

Remove from the heat and mix in the cheese. Fill the tomato shells with the chicken mixture.

Make a little flour, salt and water paste. Coat the inside rims of the tomato cases and stick on the lids. Place in a medium oven (180 degrees C) for 8–12 minutes.

In the meantime prepare the sauce. Sauté the garlic then add the rest of the ingredients

Assemble the dish by placing the tomato on a tablespoon or two of sauce. Drizzle spots of sauce around the edge and garnish with fresh coriander.

CHEF'S TIPS: Use large firm tomatoes. To speed up the preparation time and to avoid blanching, the stuffed tomatoes may be cooked by deep-frying on a metal spoon. The skins will fall away.

Ragani Ganda

ASPARAGUS SPEARS WITH RED CHILLI DRESSING

Preparation and cooking: 15 minutes   Makes four portions

Combining the subtle taste of asparagus with chilli and ginger this simple to prepare starter from Bangladesh is bursting with flavour

Ingredients

   4 - 6 Green asparagus spears per portion trimmed

The syrup
   1 red chilli de-seeded and finely diced
   4 tbs. water
   4 tbs. sugar
   2 tbs. white wine vinaigrette (1 part white wine vinegar and 2 parts olive oil)
   1 tsp. fresh ginger root peeled and grated
   Seasoning

Place asparagus in hot salted water and steam for 2 – 3 minutes

Make the syrup by stirring the sugar and water together in a frying pan over a gentle heat. Add the finely diced chilli and grated ginger. Simmer for 1-2 minutes constantly stirring. Remove from the heat. Add the vinaigrette and season.

Place the drained asparagus on the plate and drizzle over the dressing. Spot it around the rim of the plate for a professional presentation.

CHEF's tips: This versatile starter can be made with any combination of the grated vegetables you happen to have available. Slide the patties on their edge into the oil to avoid separation and damage to the shape.

Sabji ka Piaju

Mixed vegetable bhaji

Preparation: 15 minutes   Cooking: 5 minutes   Makes four portions

The flavour of fennel seeds adds zing to this popular Bangladeshi starter

Ingredients
- 200gm white cabbage shredded
- 1 medium sized onions thickly chopped
- 2 medium sized carrots grated
- ½ aubergine thinly sliced into strips
- ¼ cauliflower head finely chopped
- ½ green pepper finely chopped
- 1 desert spoon turmeric
- 1 tbs. coriander powder
- 1 fresh green chilli
- ½ tbs. cumin
- ½ tsp. fennel seeds
- Handful fresh coriander
- Salt and pepper
- 1 egg
- 4 tsp. chick pea flour
- Vegetable oil

Mix all the ingredients except the flour and oil in a bowl.

Add the flour and stir until consistency allows the mixture to be squeezed into small balls. Press each ball flat into a patty with a thickness of about 0.5cm.

Place patties into hot oil and deep fry for about 4 to 5 minutes until golden brown, turning over half way through the cooking.

Drain on kitchen paper and serve immediately. Yoghurt dressing makes a delightful dipping sauce.

Spicy Squid

FRESH BABY SQUID FRIED IN SPICED FLOUR WITH CHILLI JAM

Preparation: 25 minutes   Cooking: 15 minutes   Makes four portions

Calamari never tasted like this before! Murad's recipe combines gently spiced tempura style squid marinated in lemon and garlic with chilli and tomato sauce

Ingredients
   12 clean fresh baby squid

Marinade
   1 tsp. garlic paste
   (blend two cloves garlic with 1tbs. spoon olive oil)
   Pinch of salt
   Black pepper
   Juice of 1 lemon

Coating
   Plain flour seasoned with coriander, cumin, salt and pepper

Chilli jam
   2 fresh tomatoes roughly chopped
   2 tbs. tomato puree
   2 tbs. olive oil
   ¼ onion chopped
   ½ clove garlic chopped
   3 fresh green chillies roughly chopped
   Pinch cumin powder
   1½ tbs. sugar
   3 tbs. white vinegar
   6 tbs. water
   Pinch chilli powder

Cut off the tentacles and open up the squid tubes and place all in a bowl. Add marinade ingredients and set aside.

Prepare the chilli jam. Heat the olive oil in a hot pan. Add garlic and onion and a pinch of salt. Toss and cook until golden. Add fresh tomato, chillies, cumin, sugar and vinegar and stir. Finally add the tomato puree and reduce until the tomato is soft, stirring all the time. Add a little water if necessary to achieve a jam like consistency.

Coat the squid pieces in the spiced flour and deep fry very lightly for one minute.

Strain the chilli jam through a metal sieve and swirl on a plate.

Arrange the squid pieces on top. Drizzle spots of jam around the edge and decorate with the deep fried tentacles and basil.

CHEF's tip: The chilli jam may be stored in a jar for up to a week in the fridge.

Prawn Avocado Salad

A TIMBALE OF SPICY PRAWNS AND AVOCADO LAYERS

Preparation: 20 minutes   Cooking: 5 minutes   Makes four portions

Citrus flavours mingle with chilli and ginger in Murad's true fusion of a traditional western salad and eastern cuisine

Ingredients

Avocado layer
- 2 ripe avocados stoned, skinned and roughly chopped
- 1 shallot finely chopped
- 1 clove garlic finely chopped
- Juice of half a lemon
- 1 tomato finely chopped
- Handful fresh coriander
- Salt and pepper

Prawn layer
- 300 gm of peeled and cooked prawns
- 1 tsp. garlic and ginger paste (see page 2)
- ¼ onion finely chopped
- Pinch turmeric
- Pinch chilli powder
- 1 tbs. vegetable oil
- Mayonnaise

Place vegetable oil in a hot pan and add the prawns, salt, onion, garlic and ginger paste and toss for a couple of minutes. Remove from the heat and allow to cool. Stir in a touch of mayonnaise and set aside.

In a separate container gently squash together the avocado, lemon juice, coriander, chilli powder and garlic. Combine with the finely chopped tomato.

For each portion place a metal timbale on a plate and half fill with avocado mixture and press down firmly. Fill almost to the top with the prawn mixture and top with a very thin layer of mayonnaise.

Remove the timbale and garnish the plate with thinly sliced cucumber and fresh coriander.

CHEF'S TIP: The colours of the three layers make this a very attractive starter, but don't be too heavy-handed with the mayonnaise layer as it can mask the delicate flavours of the dish.

Cream of Butternut Squash Soup with Cumin

Preparation: 15 minutes   Cooking: 25 minutes   Makes four portions

Spices and the texture of blended squash make this one of Murad's firm favourites for a winter warmer

Ingredients

- 1 large butternut squash peeled, deseeded and sliced
- ½ onion sliced
- 1 small potato sliced
- 1 clove garlic chopped
- 1 tsp. cumin powder
- ¼ tsp. turmeric
- ½ tsp. dried coriander
- 1 litre vegetable stock
- 280ml double cream
- 100gm butter

Melt the butter in a large saucepan. Add the garlic and onion and stir until softened. Do not allow to colour. Add the squash and potato, season with salt and sauté lightly. Add the cumin, turmeric and coriander. Add the stock and simmer for 15 –20 minutes until the butternut squash is soft.

Remove from the heat and blend until smooth. Return to the pan, add the cream and warm through.

Serve with a fresh coriander leaf.

CHEF's tip: A stick blender works well and saves transferring the soup to the blender. But make sure you remove the pan from the heat first.

Cauliflower and Root Ginger Soup

Preparation: 10 minutes   Cooking: 20 minutes   Makes four portions

Delicate flavours of the cauliflower team with ginger for creamy soup without cream

Ingredients

    1 head of cauliflower chopped
    1 clove garlic chopped
    100gm butter
    ¼ onion chopped
    1inch root ginger peeled and finely chopped
    ½ litre milk
    ½ litre vegetable stock

Melt butter in large saucepan. Add onion and garlic and toss until softened, but not coloured. Add the ginger and stir. Add the cauliflower and stir. Add the stock and simmer for 10 minutes. Warm the milk and add to the cauliflower. Blitz in a blender or with a stick blender off the stove until smooth.

Serve.

CHEF's tip: Do not overcook the cauliflower as it can lose colour and flavour.

Carrot and Coriander Soup

Preparation: 15 minutes   Cooking: 20 minutes   Makes four portions

The addition of chilli and ginger gives a new twist to this tasty combination

Ingredients

- ½ kg carrots sliced
- 1 litre vegetable stock
- 1 clove garlic finely chopped
- ½ in root ginger
- 1 small potato sliced
- 280ml double cream
- 100gm butter
- 1 tsp. coriander
- 1 chilli deseeded and chopped

Melt butter in large saucepan. Add garlic, ginger and onion and toss until softened, but not coloured. Add the carrot, potato, coriander, chilli and the stock. Simmer until carrot is soft.

Remove from the heat and blend until smooth. Add the cream, warm though on the stove.

Serve garnished with fresh chopped coriander.

CHEF's tip: An optional addition to cook with the carrot is a small chopped leek.

Monkfish Vindaloo

Preparation: 10 minutes   Cooking: 45 minutes   Makes two portions

Spicy onion gravy and potatoes enhance this dense and hearty fish

Ingredients

2 monkfish fillets
1 tbs. vegetable oil
½ tsp. garlic paste
¼ tsp. turmeric
½ tsp. dry coriander
¼ tsp. methi leaves
½ tsp. chilli powder
½ tsp. tomato paste
½ tsp. vinegar
1 medium potato cubed and boiled in turmeric water
Fresh coriander

Onion gravy

3 tbs. oil
½ kg onion chopped
½ tsp. garlic paste
½ tsp. ginger paste
1 tsp. turmeric
1 litre water
Salt

Make the onion gravy by adding the onion, garlic and ginger paste and turmeric to the vegetable oil in a hot pan. Add the water, boil for 25 to 35 minutes and then remove from the heat and blend with a stick blender. Put to one side.

Heat the vegetable oil and gently fry the fillets with a touch of salt for 2 minutes each side.

In the meantime prepare the sauce by heating the oil in a large pan. Add the garlic paste, a little fresh coriander and all the powder spices and the methi leaves. Stir quickly and add the tomato paste and then the vinegar stirring continuously. Add the blended onion gravy and simmer for about a minute. Add a little water if necessary. Gently place the fish in the sauce and cook for about 6 to 8 minutes. Finally add the firm boiled potato cubes and simmer for one more minute.

Assemble the dish by placing some pieces of potato in the centre of the plate. Pile up the monkfish on top with the sauce. Drizzle more sauce around the plate and decorate with fresh coriander and chilli.

CHEF's tip: Monkfish takes a lot longer to cook than you think. If in doubt try the toothpick test. If it slides easily into the flesh the fish is done to perfection.

CHEF'S TIPS : Be very careful not to overdo the fish, which is far better eaten with that deep red colour at its heart.
Try crushed potato and fried onion as an alternative to the aubergine crush.

Seared Tuna and Aubergine Crush

Preparation: 40 minutes   Cooking: 40 minutes   Makes four portions

Marinated tuna – underdone in the middle – is teamed with the magnificent flavour of roast aubergine and the kick of green chilli. Fusion food at its best

Ingredients
  4 tuna fillets

Marinade
  Juice of two lemons
  2 tbs. olive oil
  1 tsp. garlic paste
  1 tsp. dry coriander
  ½ tsp. chilli powder

Aubergine crush
  2 large aubergines
  Handful fresh coriander chopped
  1 green chilli
  2 tomatoes chopped and deseeded
  Olive oil
  Seasoning

Dressing
  3 tbs. olive oil
  1 tbs. lemon juice
  1 tbs. fresh coriander chopped

Marinade the fish in the ingredients for at least 30 minutes. In the meantime roast the chopped aubergine in the oven. Remove from the oven and skin.

Lightly coat the tuna on one side with a dusting of flour and gently sear. Turn after a couple of minutes.

To prepare the crush place the aubergine in a blender with the other ingredients and blitz. Warm in a small pan.

Whisk the dressing together.

Assemble the dish by placing lozenges of the aubergine crush around the plate. Tilt a piece of fish in the centre. Chop some tomato and dot round the edge. Finally drizzle some dressing on top of the fish and between the tomato. Add fresh coriander. A delight on the eye and the palate!

Pan-fried Salmon with Tomato and Ginger sauce

Preparation: 15 minutes   Cooking: 10 minutes   Makes four portions

Salmon teams well with a warm Asian salad of winter vegetables

Ingredients
    4 fillets salmon

Sauce
    250 gm fresh tomatoes chopped
    ½ in ginger root grated
    1 clove garlic chopped
    1 tsp. sugar
    1 tbs. olive oil
    1 tbs. tomato puree
    Pinch of turmeric, coriander and chilli powder
    Fresh coriander

Asian winter salad
    1 carrot grated
    Cauliflower chopped
    1 onion sliced
    2 cloves garlic
    1 tbs. turmeric
    Seasoning

Gently fry the salmon in olive oil.

In the meantime prepare the sauce. Fry the garlic and ginger. Add the onion, fresh tomatoes and salt and stir. Then toss in the spices and sugar and continue to stir. Finally add the tomato puree, a drop or two of water and a handful of chopped coriander.

To prepare the salad first fry the garlic cloves with the turmeric. Add all the vegetables and toss.

Assemble the dish by piling the salad in the centre of the plate. Tilt the fish on top and swirl the sauce around the plate and a little over the fish. Decorate with tomato skin squares and coriander, or, if in season, asparagus spears.

CHEF's tip: Do check the salmon with a toothpick to ensure it is cooked to perfection.

CHEF'S TIP: Make sure the fish is cooked by testing with a toothpick. Don't miss out the fresh lemon juice – it makes all the difference!

Coconut Poached Haddock with Garlic and Coriander Mash

Preparation: 10 minutes   Cooking: 15 minutes   Makes four portions

Delicious gentle flavours highlight the sweet and textured fish

Ingredients
    4 haddock fillets
    Lemon juice

Poaching liquor
    500ml can coconut milk
    1 star anise
    1 stick cinnamon
    2 cloves garlic chopped
    1 bay leaf

Mash
    500gm potato boiled in turmeric water
    2 cloves garlic chopped
    1 tsp. oil
    Fresh chopped coriander
    Seasoning

Place the liquor ingredients in a pan and warm. Add the fish and poach for about five minutes until cooked.

To prepare the mash toss the garlic in a little hot olive oil. Add the potato, squash and toss. Add lots of fresh coriander and mix thoroughly.

To assemble, form the mash into a timbale. Place the haddock on the plate and spoon over a little of the liquor. Decorate with fine slices of tomato and steamed leek. Finally add fresh lemon juice on the top of the fish.

King Prawn Sag

Preparation: 10 minutes   Cooking: 10 minutes   Makes four portions

This is simply the best seafood to spice. And it is the most simple to prepare. Once tasted never forgotten, prawn sag is one to impress your friends!

Ingredients
- 16 uncooked king prawns peeled (but leave some small amount of shell on tail)
- 4 large handfuls of fresh spinach loosely chopped
- 2 onions chopped finely
- 3 cloves garlic chopped finely
- ½ tsp. turmeric
- 1 tbs. coriander powder
- ½ tbs. methi powder
- ¼ tsp. chilli powder
- 1 tbs. tomato paste
- Salt
- 1 tomato chopped
- Fresh coriander
- 2 tbs. vegetable oil

Drop the prawns into a pan of boiling salted water for two minutes. Put to one side.

Heat the oil in a large pan and add the garlic and onion and toss. Add the handful of fresh chopped coriander and stir. Quickly add all the spices followed by the tomato paste and the chopped fresh tomato stirring all the time. Finally add the prawns and toss swiftly. Remove from the heat and place in another dish.

Return the coated pan to the heat and quickly add the spinach and toss.

To assemble the dish, place a portion of spinach in the centre of the plate. Put four prawns around and gently pour over some sauce. Decorate with fresh coriander.

CHEF's tip: For a smooth finish add a tiny amount of water to the sauce when cooking.

Quail and Potato Curry

Preparation: 2 hours   Cooking: 50 minutes   Makes four portions

Marinated in lemon and spices before cooking gives zest to this unusual curry

Ingredients
    Eight small portions of quail
    2 medium potatoes peeled and cubed
    2 large onions sliced
    2 tomatoes chopped
    1 tbs. garlic and ginger paste (see page 2)
    2 green chillies
    1 tsp. chilli powder
    1 tsp. tumeric
    1 tsp. coriander
    1 tsp. cumin
    2 small cinnamon sticks
    2 cardamom pods
    2 bay leaves
    Handful of fresh coriander chopped
    Seasoning

Marinade
1 tbs. garlic and ginger paste (see page 2)
½ tsp. turmeric
½ tsp. coriander
½ tsp. cumin
Juice of two lemons

Marinate the quail portions for a minimum of two hours.

Quickly seal the quail in a large hot pan with 1 tbs. vegetable oil.

In another pan fry the garlic and ginger paste and onion and add a little water so that they do not burn. Add cinnamon, cardamom pods and bay leaves and season with a little salt. Continue to add a little water as needed. Add the green chillies and continue to toss the ingredients. In a small bowl mix the remaining spices in two tbs. of water and add the mixture to the pan. Stir in the tomatoes and add the potato cubes. Stir quickly and check the seasoning. Add the quail, cover and leave on a slow ring to simmer for at least 40 minutes. Check periodically and add a little water if necessary. At the last minute stir in the fresh coriander.

Serve in a large pasta bowl, piling the quail on top. Decorate with coriander.

CHEF's tip: The quail tastes even better if it has been marinated for longer – say overnight in the fridge.

CHEF's tip: Don't overcook the spinach if you want to retain its colour and flavour.

Palong Lamb

BRAISED LAMB AND SPINACH

Preparation: 45 minutes   Cooking: 2 hours   Makes four portions

Melt in the mouth lamb sits on a bed of spiced spinach

Ingredients
½ kg leg of lamb boned and cubed
200 gm. spinach
1 large onion chopped
½ tsp. garlic paste
1 tsp. turmeric
1 tsp. coriander
1 tsp. cumin
2 fresh tomatoes
2 tbs. tomato puree
Seasoning

Braising liquor
1 small onion chopped
1 tbs. garlic and ginger paste (see page 2)
1 cinnamon stick
2 bay leaves
2 cardamom pods
Pinch of turmeric
2 tsp. oil
250ml water
Seasoning

Slow cook the lamb in the liquor ingredients for about 70 minutes until the meat is soft and tender.

In a separate hot pan add a little oil and stir in the garlic paste with a little salt. Mix the spices in a couple of tablespoons of water and then add to the pan and stir. Add the tomato puree followed by the drained cooked lamb as well as four tablespoonfuls of the liquor. Stir in the fresh tomatoes. Finally add the spinach and stir until just wilted.

Serve in a large timbale with rice, tomatoes and fresh coriander.

Satraki Chicken

SPICY CHICKEN GARNISHED WITH MUSHROOMS

Preparation: 15 minutes   Cooking: 20 minutes   Makes four portions

Fast food curry that hits the spot. The addition of the mushrooms makes for a really tasty dish

Ingredients
- 500gm chicken breast fillets skinned and cubed
- 250gm button mushrooms
- 2 fresh tomatoes quartered
- 2 onions chopped
- 2 cloves garlic chopped
- 1 tsp. turmeric
- 1½ tsp. coriander
- ½ tsp. chilli powder
- 1 tsp. cumin
- Fresh coriander
- Seasoning
- 6 – 7 tbs. water

Cut the chicken breasts into thin strips and then into tiny cubes of about 0.5cm square. Put the chopped garlic and onion into a hot pan with a little vegetable oil. Add a pinch of salt and toss quickly. Mix all the dried spice in a tablespoon of water in a separate bowl and then add to the pan tossing all the time.

Add the tomatoes and then the chicken and toss to coat with the spice. Add the water and continue to turn the ingredients. After about eight minutes (when the chicken is tender) stir in the mushrooms and cook for a couple of minutes.

Serve with nan bread and fresh coriander.

CHEF's tip: This is a fairly dry curry so be careful not to add too much water.

Tulsi Chicken

CHICKEN WITH TOMATOES AND PEPPERS

Preparation: 15 minutes   Cooking: 20 minutes   Makes four portions

Red and green peppers add colour and texture to a quick chicken curry

Ingredients
    500gm chicken
    1 tbs. garlic and ginger paste (see page 2)
    1 tsp. turmeric
    1 tsp. coriander
    ½ tsp. cumin
    ½ tsp. methi leaves
    2 onions sliced
    1 green pepper sliced
    1 red pepper sliced
    ½ tsp. tomato puree
    2 large tomatoes sliced
    Fresh coriander
    2 cups water
    Seasoning

Cut the chicken into long strips and add to two tablespoons of oil in a hot pan. Seal and set aside. Mix all the dried spices in a little water in a separate bowl.

In another hot pan toss the garlic and ginger paste in a little oil followed by the salt, onions and peppers. Toss until the peppers and onions are wilted (but not really coloured). Add the spice mixture along with the tomatoes and tomato puree, tossing constantly.

Add the sautéed chicken. Mix in the water and simmer until the meat is cooked (about eight to ten minutes). Check the seasoning and add the fresh coriander.

Present in a long dish with rice of your choice.

CHEF's tip: A couple of cloves of fried garlic give this dish extra flavour.

CHEF'S Tip: Check that the lentils are not sticking to the bottom of the pan at regular intervals and add a little more water if needed.

Duck Dansak

DUCK WITH LENTILS

Preparation: 35 minutes   Cooking: 2 hours   Makes four portions

Duck gently braised with traditional curry spices and garam masala ingredients is complimented by the texture of slowly cooked lentils

Ingredients

- 1 duck cut into 16 pieces
- 2 tbs. garlic and ginger paste (see page 2)
- 2 tbs. oil
- 1 cinnamon stick
- 4 cardamom pods
- 2 bay leaves
- 250gm lentils washed and soaked
- 2 tsp. turmeric
- 2 tsp. coriander
- 1 tsp. cumin
- 1 tsp. chilli powder
- 1 litre water
- Juice of two lemons
- 2 large onions sliced
- 1 tsp. tomato puree
- 1in root ginger very finely sliced and chopped
- 2 cloves garlic chopped
- Fresh coriander
- Seasoning

Seal the duck portions in a small amount of oil and set aside on a plate to rest.

Add the onions to the pan and toss in the duck juice and oil and add a little salt. Then add the cinnamon, cardamom and bay leaves followed by ginger and garlic paste. Toss and stir with a little water to avoid burning of the spice. Cook until the onion is soft, adding more water as necessary.

Mix the powdered spices in a bowl with a little water before adding to the pan. De-glaze with a little more water to mix the flavours. Add one litre of water and the duck pieces. Cover and braise for about 50 minutes. Mix in the lentils and cook for a further 25 minutes until the lentils disappear into the sauce and the duck is falling off the bone. Add water if necessary during this time.

In a separate pan heat the oil and add the root ginger. Toss for three to four minutes until brown. Add the garlic and continue tossing and stirring. When they are both brown remove from the heat.

Add the ginger and garlic mix and a handful of chopped fresh coriander to the duck dansak and serve with rice and nan.

Lamb Shank Rogan Josh

Preparation: 15 minutes   Cooking: 3 hours   Makes four good portions

Murad's own recipe, this succulent lamb on the bone dish is a firm favourite at Chichester's Masala Gate

Ingredients
- 4 lamb shanks
- 6 tbs. oil
- 2 large onions
- 3 cinnamon sticks
- 4 cardamom pods
- 3 bay leaves
- 2 tbs. garlic and ginger paste (see page 2)
- 1 tsp. turmeric
- 2 tsp. coriander
- 1½ tsp. cumin
- ½ tsp. chilli powder
- 4 tsp. tomato puree
- 500gm can of tomatoes
- Seasoning

Cover the lamb shanks in water to which has been added the onions, ginger and garlic paste, cinnamon sticks, cardamom pods, bay leaf and salt. Cover and simmer until the lamb is soft (1½ to 2 hours).

Add the tomato puree and can of tomatoes and then fold in to the liquor with the spices. Continue to cook slowly until the lamb is falling off the bone. Check it is not sticking by adding a little water if necessary.

This dish is excellent served on a bed of mashed potato.

CHEF's tip: Place the large simmering pan on a skillet after the tomato and spices have been added to take it away from direct heat.

Tomali Chicken

TANDOORI STYLE CHICKEN

Preparation: 2½ hours   Cooking: 30 minutes   Makes four portions

A healthy option, the secret of this delicious dish is the spicy marinade. And the bright green colour of the sauce makes it a delight to behold!

Ingredients

    4 chicken breasts skinned and cut into large chunks (three per breast)

Marinade
- 1 tbs. garlic and ginger paste (see page 2)
- 200gm plain yoghurt
- ½ tsp. turmeric
- ½ tsp. coriander
- ½ tsp. cumin
- Juice of one lemon
- 1 tbs. oil

Mustard mash
- 6 large potatoes peeled and sliced
- 1 tbs. grain mustard
- 1 clove garlic chopped
- ½ tsp. turmeric
- Handful of fresh coriander chopped

Herb sauce
- Handful fresh coriander
- ½ handful fresh mint
- Handful of spinach blanched
- 4 tbs. plain yoghurt
- 4 tbs. desiccated coconut

Mix together the marinade ingredients and marinate the large chunks of chicken breast for at least two hours (or preferably overnight in the fridge).

Mix together all the ingredients of the herb sauce – except for the coconut – and blend. Fry the coconut gently and cool. Add to the herb sauce and set aside. If necessary add a bit more milk.

Remove the chicken from the marinade and grill until cooked.

Boil the potatoes in water and the turmeric. Mash. Fry the chopped garlic clove and add the mustard. Add the mashed potato and fold. Finally add the chopped coriander and gently mix. Form into lozenge shapes on a metal spoon before serving.

To assemble the dish place a tablespoonful of herb sauce on each plate and smear. Add the mash lozenge and place the chicken on top.

CHEF's tip: to give the dish its traditional pink/red colour add a tablespoonful of cooked beetroot blended with a little oil to the marinade.

Bringal Bhaji

AUBERGINE BHAJI

Preparation: 20 minutes   Cooking: 15 minutes   Makes four portions

A vegetarian's delight, this aubergine and tomato dish is a favourite with everyone

Ingredients
- 2 aubergines sliced and quartered
- 1 large onion chopped
- 2 fresh tomatoes chopped
- Oil
- Pinch mustard seeds
- Pinch cumin seeds
- 1 tsp. turmeric
- 1 tsp. coriander
- ½ tsp. chilli powder
- ½ tbs. garlic and ginger paste (see page 2)
- Fresh coriander
- Seasoning

Put a little oil in a large frying pan. When hot add the mustard and cumin seed and toss until they crackle. Add the onion and cook until soft and transparent. Add salt and pepper to taste. Add the garlic and ginger paste, all the other spices and the tomatoes and stir.

Deep fry the aubergines in a separate pan or fryer for two minutes. Drain on paper and put in the pan with the other ingredients. Add 2 tbs. of water and stir.

Serve with fresh coriander.

CHEF'S TIP: Do not fry the aubergines for too long. They should be soft with just a hint of browning.

Vegetable Sambar

SPICY VEGETABLES AND LENTILS

Preparation: 20 minutes Cooking: 65 minutes   Makes four portions

Roasted and ground spicy seeds and dried chilli give a real pep to lentils and vegetables

Ingredients
- 250gm lentil
- 250gm mixed vegetables blanched
- 2 small onions
- 1 fresh tomato chopped
- ½ tsp coriander seed
- ½ tsp. cumin seed
- ¼ tsp fenugreek seeds
- 2 dried red chillies chopped
- 1 tbs. garlic and ginger paste (see page 2)
- 2 tbs. oil
- ¼ tbs. turmeric
- ¼ tbs. chilli powder
- ½ tbs. coriander
- ¼ tbs. cumin
- 3 tbs. tamarind juice or the juice of 1 lemon
- ½ tbs. sugar
- Fresh coriander
- Seasoning

Fry a quarter of a chopped onion until transparent. Add a pinch of turmeric and place in a pan with the lentils. Cover well with water and boil for 45 minutes or until soft. Set aside this dal.

In the meantime heat a frying pan and add the coriander, cumin, fenugreek and mustard seeds and dried chilli. When they have "popped" remove from the heat. Grind the cooled seeds to powder.

To assemble fry a small onion in two tbs. oil until brown. Add the spices and garlic and ginger paste. Stir in the vegetables and tomato.

Add the dal followed by 6 tbs. water. Stir in the tamarind or lemon juice.

Finally add the ground roasted spice seeds and serve with fresh coriander.

CHEF'S TIP: Make sure the pan is really hot before adding the seeds.

CHEF'S TIP: Maris Piper potatoes make the best vegetable curry. They retain their shape when chopped and cooked.

Mixed Vegetable Curry

TRADITIONAL CURRY OF SEASONAL VEGETABLES

Preparation: 20 minutes   Cooking: 25 minutes   Makes four portions

A colourful accompaniment to any meal or served as a vegetarian option, this dish uses whatever vegetables are available

Ingredients

2 medium sized onions chopped
4 fresh tomatoes chopped
2 potatoes peeled, chopped and blanched
2 carrots chopped and blanched
¼ cauliflower in florets blanched
¼ butternut squash chopped and blanched
Handful of runner beans chopped and blanched
150gm frozen or fresh peas
2 tbs. oil
Pinch of cumin seed
Pinch of mustard seed

3 bay leaves
Cinnamon stick
2 cardamom pods
1 tbs. garlic and ginger paste (see page 2)
1 tsp. turmeric
2 tsp. coriander
1 tsp. cumin
1 tsp. chilli powder
600ml water
Seasoning

Heat the oil in a frying pan. Add the cumin seed and mustard seed and toss until they crackle. Add the cinnamon, bay leaves and cardamom followed by the onions and a pinch of salt. Stir continuously until the onion is very soft.

Add the garlic and ginger paste and the tomatoes followed by all the spices and stir in 2 tsp. water so that the spices do not burn. This mixture is the basis of the curry.

Place in a large pan and add all the drained vegetables. Stir and add 600ml of water.

Simmer for ten minutes or until the potato is cooked. Serve with fresh coriander.

Vegetable Kedgeree

VEGETABLES COOKED WITH RICE AND LENTILS

Preparation: 60 minutes   Cooking: 30 minutes   Makes four portions

A hearty, filling meal in itself, this lentil rice dish is also extremely good with curry rather than rice

Ingredients

- 200gm lentils
- 400gm rice
- 1 small onion chopped
- Bunch of green beans
- 5 or 6 cauliflower florets
- 1 carrot chopped into batons
- 1 potato chopped
- 3 tbs. frozen peas
- 1/8 butternut squash chopped
- 1½ tbs. garlic and ginger paste (see page 2)
- 2 green chilli peppers
- Cinnamon stick
- 3 cardamom pods
- 2 bay leaves
- ½ tbs. turmeric
- 1 tbs. coriander
- ½ tbs. chilli powder
- ¼ tbs. cumin
- 1,200ml water
- 2 tbs. ghee or clarified butter
- 1 tbs. wholegrain mustard
- Seasoning

Prepare the vegetables and leave to soak in cold water for 40 minutes.

Soak the rice and lentils together in water for 35 minutes.

Heat the ghee in a large frying pan until hot. Add the cardamom, cinnamon and bay leaves followed by the onion and salt to taste. Stir rapidly until the onion is soft, but not brown.

Add the ginger and garlic paste and all the spices. Stir in the wholegrain mustard. Quickly stir in 2 tbs. of water so the spices do not burn. Add all the vegetables and the soaked rice and lentils. Sautee until all the water has gone.

Transfer to a large lidded saucepan and add 1,200ml of water. Cover with the lid and leave on a medium heat for 15 minutes. Serve.

CHEF's TIPS: For added flavour use vegetable stock rather than water. Add a little milk with the water to soften the spice colour.

Breads

CHAPATI, PURI AND PARATHA

Preparation: 30 minutes Cooking: 5 minutes   Makes 3 paratha, 4 puri or 4 chapati

Basic ingredients and preparation are the same for chapati, puri and paratha

Ingredients

> 350gm plain flour
> Pinch salt
> 170ml cold water

Mix the water into the flour bit by bit until a doughy consistency is reached. Knead the dough in the bowl. Here's the secret: place the dough in the fridge for 15 to 20 minutes so that the gluten has time to work.

Chapati

This most staple of foods is easy to make and is fat-free. Flour a board and divide the dough into four. Shape into rounds and roll into circles of 9 –10cm in diameter as thin as possible. Place one by one into a hot non-stick pan and keep turning over for a couple of minutes until cooked. Remove, fold over and serve.

Puri

Prepare in the same way as chapati. Cook by dropping gently into hot oil and turn over once. Remove and drain on kitchen paper.

Paratha

Using the same dough divide into three. Roll out and carefully place one teaspoon of oil along the centre. Roll up into a long sausage and then roll this round and round to resemble a Catherine wheel. Roll flat again. Cook in a non-stick pan. When coloured turn over and add a tiny amount of oil and return to the pan.

CHEF's tip: Paratha makes a great accompaniment when stuffed with vegetables. Stuff before rolling into the sausage shape with blanched or leftover cooked vegetables!

Boiled Rice

Plain basmati

Preparation: 4 minutes
Cooking: 15 minutes

Perfect boiled rice has to be fluffy and separated. Follow Murad's easy steps to get it right every time

Ingredients
     150 gm per person basmati rice
     Pan full of water and a pinch salt

Firstly wash the rice four or five times to remove all the excess starch.

Put a pinch of salt in a large pan of water and bring to the boil.

Add the rice and boil for approximately 10 minutes.

Check the rice to see if it is slightly "al dente" then strain in a colander.

Place back in the pan and cover. Return to a very low heat for a minute. The set aside for five minutes off the heat.

**CHEF's tip: The secret for separated grains of rice is the thorough washing to remove the starch that can stick the rice together. It is worth the effort.
If you are frightened of burning the rice when you place it back on the stove, put the pan in a non-stick frying pan to take it away from direct heat.**

Pilau Rice
Fried spicy basmati

Preparation: 6 minutes
Cooking: 40 minutes
Serves four

When it comes to a complement to a good curry, this is the rice of choice

Ingredients
400gm (150 gm per person) basmati rice
1 tsp. garlic and ginger paste (see page 2)
2 cardamom pods
cinnamon stick
1 bay leaf
2 tsp. ghee or clarified butter
seasoning to taste
¼ onion chopped
tiny bit of saffron (optional)
700ml hot water

Wash and strain the rice four or five times and put on one side. Put ghee in a pan on the heat and add the onion. When slightly soft add the garlic and ginger paste and stir. It should not be allow to colour. Add all the spices except the saffron and toss with the onion. Add the rice and seasoning and continue stirring for about three minutes. Add the hot water. Place a lid on the pan. Turn to a medium heat and cook on a rolling boil. Do NOT open the lid.

After 15 minutes remove from the heat and allow to rest. Do NOT remove the lid! After 20 minutes take off the lid for the best pilau rice you have ever tasted! For a variation add lemon or mushrooms or bits and pieces of left over vegetables with the rice when frying.

CHEF'S tips : If you like the yellow colour favoured by some put a small amount of saffron into a cup of water and microwave for one minute. Add this to the pan with the other water before covering and boiling.

All Spiced Apple Crumble

Preparation: 40 minutes   Cooking: 50 minutes
Serves eight (four and plenty of leftovers!)

Apple crumble with a spicy twist all sitting in a pastry case. A serious pudding.

Ingredients

Sweet shortcrust pastry
- 250gm plain flour
- 125gm butter
- Pinch salt
- 2 eggs
- 65gm castor sugar
- Zest whole lemon

Crumble
- 250gm plain flour
- 125gm sugar
- 125gm butter (cut into small pieces)
- Zest of lemon
- Pinch ginger powder
- Pinch cinnamon powder

Apple filling
- 4 sliced apples (Granny Smith preferred)
- Juice of 1 lemon
- 1 tsp. cinnamon powder
- ½ tsp. ginger powder
- ½ tsp. all spice 150 g sultanas
- 100gm soft brown sugar

Prepare the pastry by creaming the butter and sugar. Add the eggs carefully one by one. Then fold in the flour bit by bit. Add the lemon and a pinch of salt. Form into a ball and put in the fridge whilst you prepare the crumble and the apples.

For the crumble, rub the flour together with the small pieces of butter into small pieces. Add the sugar, lemon zest and spice and stir.

Thinly slice the apple and add the other ingredients to coat the fruit.

Roll out the pastry and line a 12in flan case (with removable base). Fill with apple mixture and top liberally with the crumble. Place in the middle shelf of the oven and bake for 45–50 minutes at 180°C.

CHEF's tip:
To get a deep filled crumble build up the pastry by letting it coat the outside of the flan case.

CHEF's tips: BE VERY CAREFUL WHEN CARAMELISING SUGAR. It has a very high boiling temperature and burns can be serious. This dessert is even better if left in the fridge for longer than 4 hours (overnight is best). It will keep for up to three days.

Gajarka Halwa

SOFT CARROT PUDDING

Preparation: 20 minutes Cooking: 15 minutes   Serves four to six

The Asian equivalent of carrot cake without the cake, this is a quick dessert with which to impress your guests!

Ingredients

    500gm grated carrot
    500ml milk or cream
    1 tsp. cardamom pod crushed (optional)
    ½ tsp. cinnamon powder
    2 tbs. ghee or clarified butter
    2 tbs. raisins or sultanas or a mixture of both
    200gm castor sugar (less to your taste)

Boil the carrot and milk (or cream) until the carrot is cooked and the milk absorbed. Add the sugar. In a separate frying pan toss the sultanas and raisins with the ghee until the fruit is soft and tender. Add to the carrot mixture. Stir in the spices.

Place the mixture in small timbale moulds and cool. Serve with a scoop of vanilla ice cream.

Index

Apple Crumble (All-spiced) 50
Asparagus with red chilli 4
Aubergine Bhaji 40
Breads 46
Bringal Bhaji 40
Butternut Squash Soup with cumin 12
Cardamom Crème Brulée 53
Carrot and Coriander Soup 15
Carrot pudding 59
Cauliflower and Root Ginger Soup 14
Chapati 46
Chicken with mushrooms 30
Chicken Satraki 30
Chicken Tandoori style 38
Chicken Tomali 38
Chicken with tomatoes and peppers 32
Chicken Tulsi 32
Cinnamon Panna Cotta 56
Duck Dansak 35
Gajarka Halwa 59
Garlic and ginger paste 2
Goti Mahal 2
Haddock poached with coconut 23
King Prawn Sag 24
Lamb with spinach 29
Lamb Palong 29
Lamb Shank Rogan Josh 36
Lentils and vegetables 41
Mango Mousse 54
Monkfish Vindaloo 16
Paratha 46
Prawn Avocado Salad 10
Puri 46
Quail and Potato Curry 26
Ragani Ganda 4
Rice Boiled 48
Rice Pilau 49
Sabji ka Piaju 7
Sag Roll 1
Salmon Pan-fried with Tomato
    and Ginger Sauce 20
Spicy Squid 8
Spinach and potato roll 1
Tomatoes stuffed with spicy chicken 2
Tuna (Seared) and Aubergine Crush ... 19
Vegetable Bhaji 7
Vegetable Curry 43
Vegetable Kedgeree 44
Vegetable Sambar 41